The Well-Temper Violin

By Michael McLean

© 1992 Summy-Birchard Music
division of Summy-Birchard Inc.
All rights reserved. Printed in U.S.A.

0-87487-434-3
1 3 5 7 9 8 6 4 2

Summy Birchard Inc.
exclusively distributed by
Warner Bros. Publications Inc.
265 Secaucus Road
Secaucus, NJ 07096-2037

Design: Aean Pinheiro

FOREWORD

In the early 18th century, J.S. Bach composed his "Well-Tempered Klavier" with two purposes in mind; to show that the newly developed well-tempered system of tuning would support pieces composed in every key and also as a pedagogical treatise on fugal counterpoint for his children.

The "Well-Tempered Violin" is inspired by these concepts. These pieces were composed in order to introduce every key to the young violinist. This is not a system to introduce reading, but rather a system that will strengthen reading skills.

Within this framework, the popular dances and forms of the Baroque era are represented throughout the manuscript. A simple and straight-forward text explains each piece and hopefully will enlighten and inform the student about this important repertoire.

It is suggested, especially further into this book, that the teacher preface each piece with the corresponding scale and arpeggio.

CONTENTS

1. CANON in C Major

A. A canon is a musical composition where a melody in one voice is imitated in another voice.

B. The structure of this piece is based on sonata form. There are three basic sections in Sonata form: Exposition, Development, and Recapitulation.

1. *EXPOSITION.* This is the first section in sonata form where the various themes are presented or exposed. Here, the main theme consists of the first two measures.
2. *DEVELOPMENT.* This section follows the exposition and is usually marked by a double bar. Here, the themes that were presented in the exposition are developed and put back together in different ways.
3. *RECAPITULATION.* In this third section, the exposition is loosely repeated and remains in C major.

C. Melodic inversion happens when a previously stated melody is turned upside down, keeping the same intervals but in the opposite direction. Compare the first two measures of the piece and the first two measures of the development.

Development
(melodic inversion)

Recapitulation

2. TRIO SONATA in A minor

The trio sonata traditionally consists of two upper voices of similar range and basso continuo (cello and harpsichord). Very often the upper voices present the same melodies and imitate each other. The basso continuo has the role of accompaniment.

The composers who wrote trio sonatas lived in the period of history called the Baroque Era (1600-1750). The trio sonata was a very popular form and composers such as Bach, Handel, Corelli, and Vivaldi wrote many.

3. FUGUE in G Major

The fugue is another composition developed in the Baroque Era. Here, the voices enter one by one and present the same theme in related keys (tonic, dominant, etc.). Although there is no rigid form for the fugue, it is always based on imitative counterpoint. The following terms help one understand the structure of the fugue.

1. **FUGUE SUBJECT** - the main theme of the fugue
2. **ANSWER** - the main theme of the fugue but in a related key (dominant) and usually the 2nd and 4th entrances.
3. **COUNTERSUBJECT** - the theme that is played at the same time as the subject or counter to the subject.
4. **EXPOSITION** - the section found from the very beginning until all voices have presented the fugue subject.
5. **COUNTERPOINT** - two or more different melodies played at the same time.
6. **EPISODE** - the scetions in the fugue where the full subject is not present but often where fragments of the subject are used imitatively.
7. **PEDALPOINT** - sustained note usually in the bass and changing chords in the upper voices.

Allegro

Exposition

M. McLean

Pedal Point

4. CHORALE PRELUDE in E minor
"Christ Lag in Todes Banden"

The chorale prelude is an organ piece that uses a chorale tune (a Protestant hymn tune).
The composition starts independently of the chorale but throughout, phrases of the chorale
are presented within the texture of the prelude. Since these pieces were originally performed
in the Lutheran church, the congregation would sing when the chorale was played.

Christ Lag in Todes Banden is German for Christ lay in Death's Bonds, a very famous
Easter chorale.

M. McLean

5. PERPETUAL MOTION in F Major

A perpetual motion is a piece using the same rapid motion without stopping. The most famous perpetual motion is probably the one by Paganini, "Moto Perpetuo".

This perpetual motion is also a canon which only waits one beat before the next voice enters.

M. McLean

6. BOURRÉE in D minor

The bourrée is a 17th century French dance in a quick duple meter (2/2 or ¢) with a quick upbeat on beat four. This quick upbeat is usually found throughout the dance.

Allegro

M. McLean

7. VOLUNTARY in D Major

The voluntary is an English organ piece based on imitative counterpoint. This composition was usually improvised and performed between the reading of the Psalms and the 1st Lesson. Jeramiah Clarke wrote the famous "Trumpet Voluntary".

M. McLean

8. SICILIANO in B minor

During the 17th and 18th centuries, the dance of choice in Sicily was the Siciliano. This dance was written in 6/8 or 12/8 meter (or 6/4 here) and has a soft, lyrical melody with dotted rhythms.

Andante Affettuoso

M. McLean

9. MINUET in B Flat Major

Jean Baptiste Lully was said to have composed the first minuet around 1650 in France for King Louis XIV who danced to the first minuet. This French dance is in a moderate 3/4 and usually written with a phrase every two measures. The pulse is on the downbeat.

M. McLean

10. SARABANDE in G minor

The place of origin for the sarabande was the New World, namely Mexico. From here, the dance was taken to Spain in the early 16th century and matured in France and England in the 17th and 18th centuries. The sarabande is in a slow triple meter and in a dignified style with a stress on the 2nd beat.

CANON AT THE 5TH - a canon where the 2nd voice imitates the first voice five tones higher or lower.

M. McLean

11. COUNTRY DANCE in A Major

The country dance is usually based on English folk melodies which are simple and happy in nature with a marked rhythm.

M. McLean

12. BADINERIE in F Sharp minor

The badinerie is a dance-like piece that is light and witty in character and is sometimes found in the Baroque Suite (a grouping of dances).

Allegro Giocoso

M. McLean

13. CANON in E Flat Major

A. A canon is a musical composition where a melody in one voice is imitated in another voice.

B. The structure of this piece is based on sonata form. There are three basic sections in sonata form: Exposition, Development, and Recapitulation.

1. *EXPOSITION.* This is the first section in sonata form where the various themes are presented or exposed. Here, the main theme consists of the first two measures.
2. *DEVELOPMENT.* This section follows the exposition and is usually marked by a double bar. Here, the themes that were presented in the exposition are developed and put back together in different ways.
3. *RECAPITULATION.* In this third section, the exposition is loosely repeated and remains in C major.

C. Melodic inversion happens when a previously stated melody is turned upside down, keeping the same intervals but in the opposite direction. Compare the first two measures of the piece and the first two measures of the development.

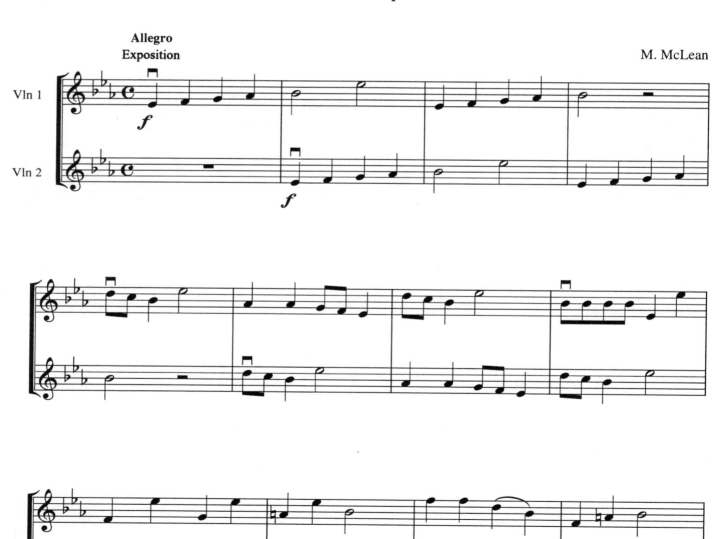

Development
(melodic inversion)

Recapitulation

14. RICECAR in C minor

The ricecar is the form from which the fugue eventually developed. It is also imitative but uses a series of subjects which lack rhythmic and melodic individuality. The ricecar was popular in the 16th and 17th centuries.

M. McLean

15. DA CAPO ARIA in E Major
Section "A"

The "da capo aria" was very popular from 1650-1750. this type of aria was found in either the opera or the oratorio and has two sections with a repeat of the first section, making the form ABA. The middle section is usually in a different but related key.

TUTTI - full orchestra without the vocal solo.
SOLO - the vocal solo with lighter orchestral accompaniment.

M. McLean

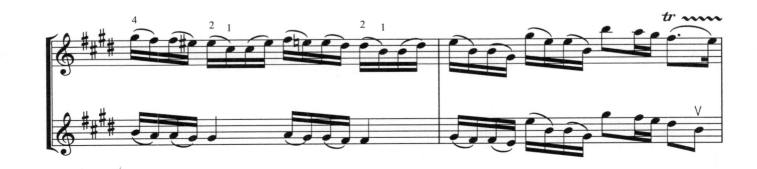

16. DA CAPO ARIA in C Sharp minor
Section "B"

The "da capo aria" was very popular from 1650-1750. this type of aria was found in either the opera or the oratorio and has two sections with a repeat of the first section, making the form ABA. The middle section is usually in a different but related key.

TUTTI - full orchestra without the vocal solo.
SOLO - the vocal solo with lighter orchestral accompaniment.

17. GAVOTTE in A Flat Major

The gavotte is a French dance in a moderate 4/4 meter with an upbeat of two quarter notes.
The phrases in the gavotte begin and end in the middle of the measure. Again, Lully made it
popular in his ballets and operas and this dance eventually became popular all over Europe.

M.McLean

18. WALTZ in F minor

The waltz originated in Austria around 1800 and developed from the Austrian peasant dance, the Ländler. The waltz quickly became very popular since the dance partners were allowed to embrace one another. This dance is in a moderate 3/4 time with the characteristic off beats on two and three.

M. McLean

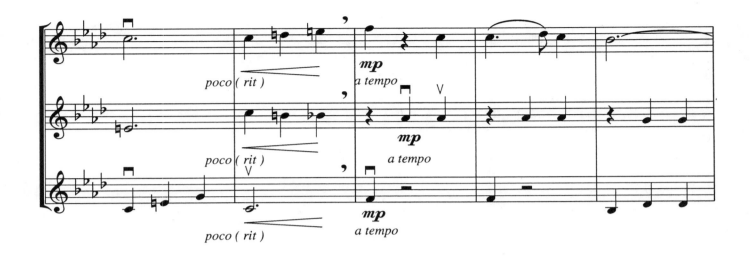

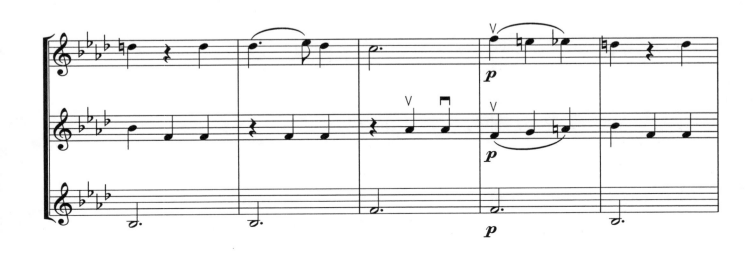

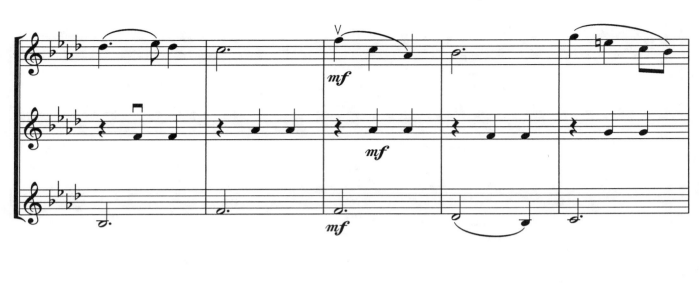

19. DIVERTISSEMENT in B Major

The function of the divertissement in the 18th century was primarily to entertain. This light instrumental work was used for such occasions as royal dinners, outdoor concerts, or music used between scenes in a play or opera.

M. McLean

20. CHORALE in G Sharp minor

Chorales are hymns sung in the German Protestant church. Martin Luther was very important in developing this tradition by gathering sacred texts in German and using tuneful secular songs for the melody. These chorales were eventually arranged for four voice parts, soprano, alto, tenor, and bass with Bach's settings being the most popular.

M. McLean / BACH

21. AIR in D Flat Major

In 17th and 18th Century France, the air was composed as a simple song with the light accompaniment of perhaps a lute. It was also found in the operas of the day. In England, ayre was the equivalent term, with Purcell and Locke writing many.

M. McLean

22. CANON (at the 5th) in B Flat minor

M. McLean

23. DUET in F Sharp Major

The duet is simply a composition for two performers in which the parts are both equal.

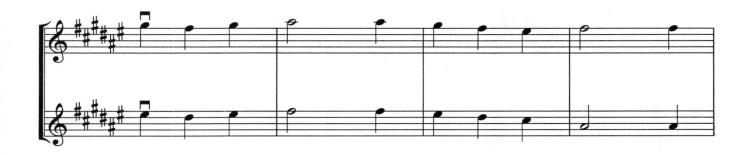

24. FOLK SONG in E Flat minor
"Twinkle"

Need I say anything about Twinkle?

Traditional